LEARN TOGETHER

TEST YOUR REASONING 1

Home tests in basic reasoning skills

Words, diagrams and shapes

Roy Childs

Illustrated by Graham Butler

MACMILLAN
CHILDREN'S BOOKS

Just for Fun!

Before you start

This book is designed for your child to test his or her reasoning ability at home. A detailed introduction is given in the tinted pull-out section between pages 14 and 15. The answer key is also in this section. In case you want your child to work through the tests without access to the answers, you can pull out the tinted section carefully and keep it separately. (You may have to push back the staples slightly.)

So, before your child starts work, turn to the middle and read the suggestions on how to use the book.

First published in the Practise Together series 1987 by Pan Books Ltd

Published 1993 as *Junior Test Your Reasoning*
by Pan Macmillan Children's Books

This edition published 1996 by Macmillan Children's Books
a division of Macmillan Publishers Limited
25 Eccleston Place, London SW1W 9NF
and Basingstoke

Associated companies throughout the world

ISBN 0 330 34947 3

Text copyright © Roy Childs 1987
Illustrations copyright © Graham Butler 1987

The moral right of the author has been asserted.

3 5 7 9 8 6 4

This book is sold subject to the condition that it shall not,
by way of trade or otherwise, be lent, re-sold, hired out,
or otherwise circulated without the publisher's prior consent
in any form of binding or cover other than that in which
it is published and without a similar condition including this
condition being imposed on the subsequent purchaser.

Whilst the advice and information in this book are believed to
be true and accurate at the time of going to press, neither the
author nor the publisher can accept any legal responsibility or
liability for any errors or omissions that may be made.

Photoset by Parker Typesetting Service, Leicester
Printed and bound in Great Britain by Henry Ling Ltd,
The Dorset Press, Dorchester

Suggestions for activities to help your reasoning skills

In everyday life we are always solving problems. Deciding which is the best bike to buy or the quickest way to get to a friend's house involves reasoning and problem solving. Some of us are better than others at certain kinds of reasoning but usually not at all kinds of reasoning. The test in this booklet might show that you find words easier to deal with than diagrams, for example. If you want to try to improve your reasoning skills you have to practise them. It is probably true that solving any kind of problem helps you to develop your general reasoning, but some activities are better than others for developing certain kinds of reasoning. Below are some suggestions for activities which involve solving problems which might help to improve your reasoning skills.

1.   Verbal Reasoning Skills

Any games that make you more familiar with words are useful. Crosswords, hangman or scrabble are all good examples. Try to play more games which concentrate on words. Traditional English exercises as done in school help a lot, too.

2.   Non-Verbal Reasoning Skills

Games involving logic, sequences, and classification can all be useful. Card games, more and more difficult jigsaw puzzles, books of puzzles, chess, draughts, and Kim's game all require you to reason in ways other than just with words.

3.   Spatial Reasoning Skills

Playing games like 'I spy' can help you notice differences and similarities in the world around you. Noticing how they change when looked at from different angles, or playing with shapes, cubes, Lego, or playing 'GO', or card games such as 'pairs' all may help you to develop better spatial reasoning skills.

The above suggestions may help you to improve your reasoning skills in the different areas tested by this booklet but, just as valuable, is practice in all the subjects and skills you learn at school. Think about some of these, too, and practise them when you can.

Unit One

Look at this picture.

A bat
B (cat)
C dog
D came

Can you see that we have circled the word CAT? This is the word that stands for the picture.

Now do these questions by putting a circle around the word which stands for the picture.

Test One starts here

1. A dog
    B ride
    C horse
    D house

2. A knife
    B nice
    C kennel
    D night

3. A boy
    B sea
    C sink
    D boat

4. A upper
    B umbrella
    C parachute
    D under

5. A ball
    B boy
    C back
    D bald

6.
    A plan
    B plate
    C pepper
    D piece

7. A wheel
    B test
    C train
    D tide

8. A buckle
    B blade
    C banana
    D butter

9. A television
    B telephone
    C temper
    D telescope

10. A walking
    B resting
    C riding
    D running

Now look at this box.

> Cross the <u>road</u>
> A river
> B (street)
> C grass
> D house

The word road is underlined on the top line. You must circle one of the choices labelled A, B, C or D which means almost the same. The answer here is B – street.

Now do these.

11. The <u>big</u> dog
    A frightening
    B large
    C furry
    D little

12. She <u>talked</u> quietly
    A spoke
    B laughed
    C shouted
    D walked

13. the <u>even</u> ground
    A odd
    B rough
    C stony
    D level

14. a <u>brave</u> girl
    A silly
    B stupid
    C thoughtless
    D courageous

15. the cup <u>smashed</u>
    A filled
    B broke
    C spilled
    D drank

16. in the <u>gloom</u>
    A light
    B glare
    C darkness
    D glut

17. <u>pleased</u> to see you
    A glad
    B worried
    C upset
    D wanted

18. pull the <u>plug</u>
    A cotton-wool
    B chain
    C stopper
    D rope

19. to <u>trudge</u> home
    A plod
    B hop
    C walk
    D run

20. to <u>turn</u> around
    A run
    B talk
    C teach
    D spin

Unit One Score   1–10 [   ]   11–20 [   ]   Total [   ]

5

Unit Two

Look at these words.

cow, mouse, cat, ___?___

They are all animals but there is one missing. Which of these next four words goes best with the words above?

boat   plane   (dog)   grass

The answer is the dog because it is also an animal. We have put a ring around it to show it is the right answer. Now try this example.

red, green, blue, ___?___

apple   yellow   snow   pot

You should have put a ring around 'yellow' because it is a colour like red, green and blue. If you got it wrong ask someone to explain, otherwise begin the test.

Test Two starts here

1. | apple, banana, plum, ___?___ |
   |---|

   pear   carrot   leaf   knife

2. | shoulder, elbow, hip, ___?___ |
   |---|

   nose   ear   knee   door

3. | Monday, Wednesday, Sunday, ___?___ |
   |---|

   Summer   Tuesday   holiday   tomorrow

4. | breakfast, tea, supper, ___?___ |
   |---|

   sausage   jam   plank   dinner

5. hear, smell, see, ___?___

kneel   loud   feel   bright

6. talk, sing, whisper, ___?___

speak   watch   listen   play

7. hop, leap, jump, ___?___

talk   stroll   ride   spring

8. wind, gale, hurricane, ___?___

breeze   wave   blow   seaside

9. bowl, trough, cup, ___?___

table   basin   plank   drink

10. table, chair, sofa, ___?___

room   stool   bed   floor

11. river, brook, stream, ___?___

ocean   creek   boat   flow

12. gorge, stuff, fill, ___?___

run   empty   feed   cram

13. vast, large, huge, ___?___

immense   barrel   short   down

14. envelope, letter, postman, ___?___

boot   stamp   send   system

15. shoe, boot, sock, ___?___

glove   hand   sandal   ankle

16. magazine, journal, comic, ___?___

newspaper   pages   learn   printed

17. race, contest, competition, ___?___

fire   team   run   match

18. anger, fury, wrath, ___?___

sleep   happy   wet   rage

19. inactive, lazy, sluggish, ___?___

fat   idle   fast   snail

20. bumpy, uneven, irregular, ___?___

rough   yellow   square   paper

Unit Two 1–20 Score

Unit Three

Look at these words:

>   big ⟶ little   tall ⟶ short

The pairs go together because they are opposites. 'Little' is the opposite of 'big' and 'short' is the opposite of 'tall'. In this test the questions will look like this:

>   big ⟶ little   as tall ⟶ | fat (short) long big |

You can see that we have circled 'short' to show that it goes with 'tall' in the same way as 'little' goes with 'big'.

Now try this example and put a ring around your choice before reading on.

>   food ⟶ eat   as water ⟶ | swim run drink pour |

You should have put a ring around 'drink'. We eat food and we drink water. You can swim in water but it is not the right answer because 'water' and 'swim' do not go together **in the same way** as 'food' and 'eat'. If you are not sure what to do ask someone to explain. Otherwise begin the test.

Test Three starts here

1. glove ⟶ hand   as sock ⟶ | scarf knee foot ankle |

2. pea ⟶ vegetable as pear ⟶ | apple two fruit grass |

3. nose ⟶ smell   as ear ⟶ | see hear feel lobe |

4. light ⟶ day   as dark ⟶ | black night bright sight |

5. teacher ⟶ school as nurse ⟶ | hospital   bed   hat   ward

6. front ⟶ rear as order ⟶ | chaos   clean   obey   postal

7. scream ⟶ yell as shun ⟶ | shout   shield   after   avoid

8. sleeve ⟶ arm as collar ⟶ | neck   foot   knee   shoulder

9. jog ⟶ sprint as trot ⟶ | stroll   trip   gallop   trek

10. grass ⟶ green as snow ⟶ | dwarf   white   melt   cold

11. happy ⟶ sad as laugh ⟶ | cry   grin   play   shout

12. cap ⟶ head as bracelet ⟶ | neck   wrist   shoulder   ring

13. fox ⟶ fur   as sparrow ⟶ | fly air feather bird |

14. circle ⟶ wheel as sphere ⟶ | ball banana ballroom bounce |

15. hole ⟶ heap   as valley ⟶ | mountain trees river dig |

16. smooth ⟶ texture as red ⟶ | light danger blood colour |

17. tree ⟶ plant   as mouse ⟶ | animal runs cheese hole |

18. degree ⟶ temperature as minute ⟶ | time amount small hot |

19. brick ⟶ house   as tree ⟶ | leaves branches plant forest |

20. dew ⟶ frost   as rain ⟶ | drop hail cloud wet |

Unit Three Score 1–20

Unit Four

Look at these shapes. They are in a special order.

Which of these comes next?

The answer is A which has been circled. The series goes 3, 2, 3 and so the next one must be 2. Now try this example:

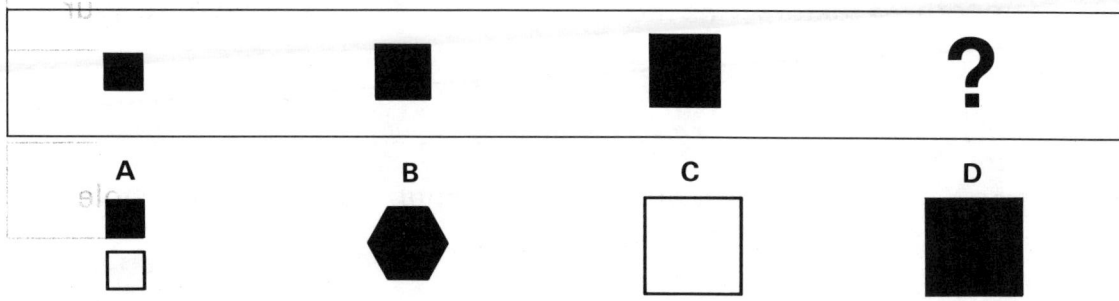

You should have circled D – the big black square. If you got it wrong ask someone to explain. Otherwise begin the test.

Test Four starts here

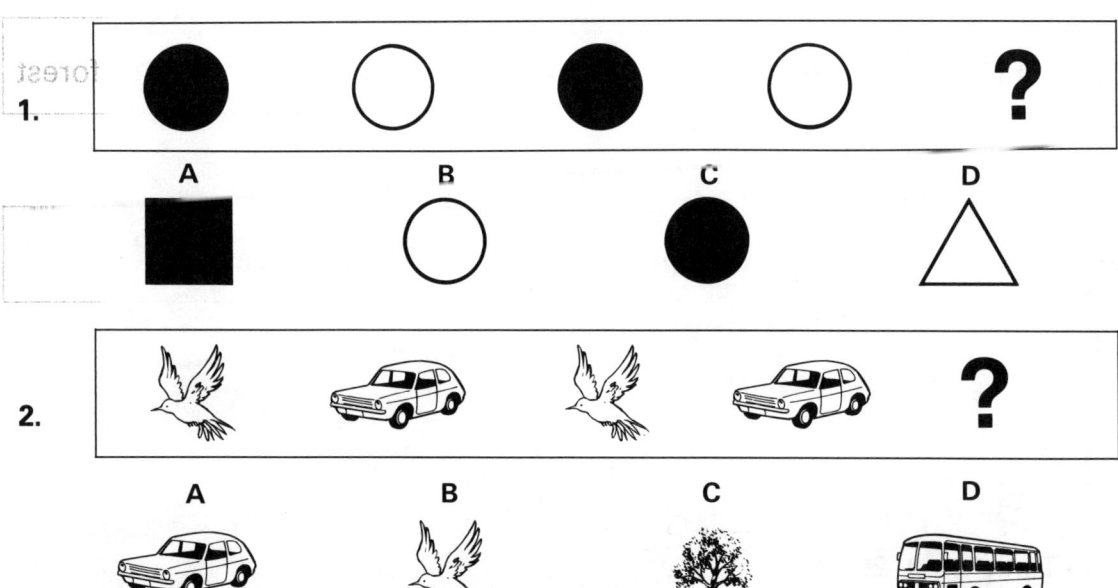

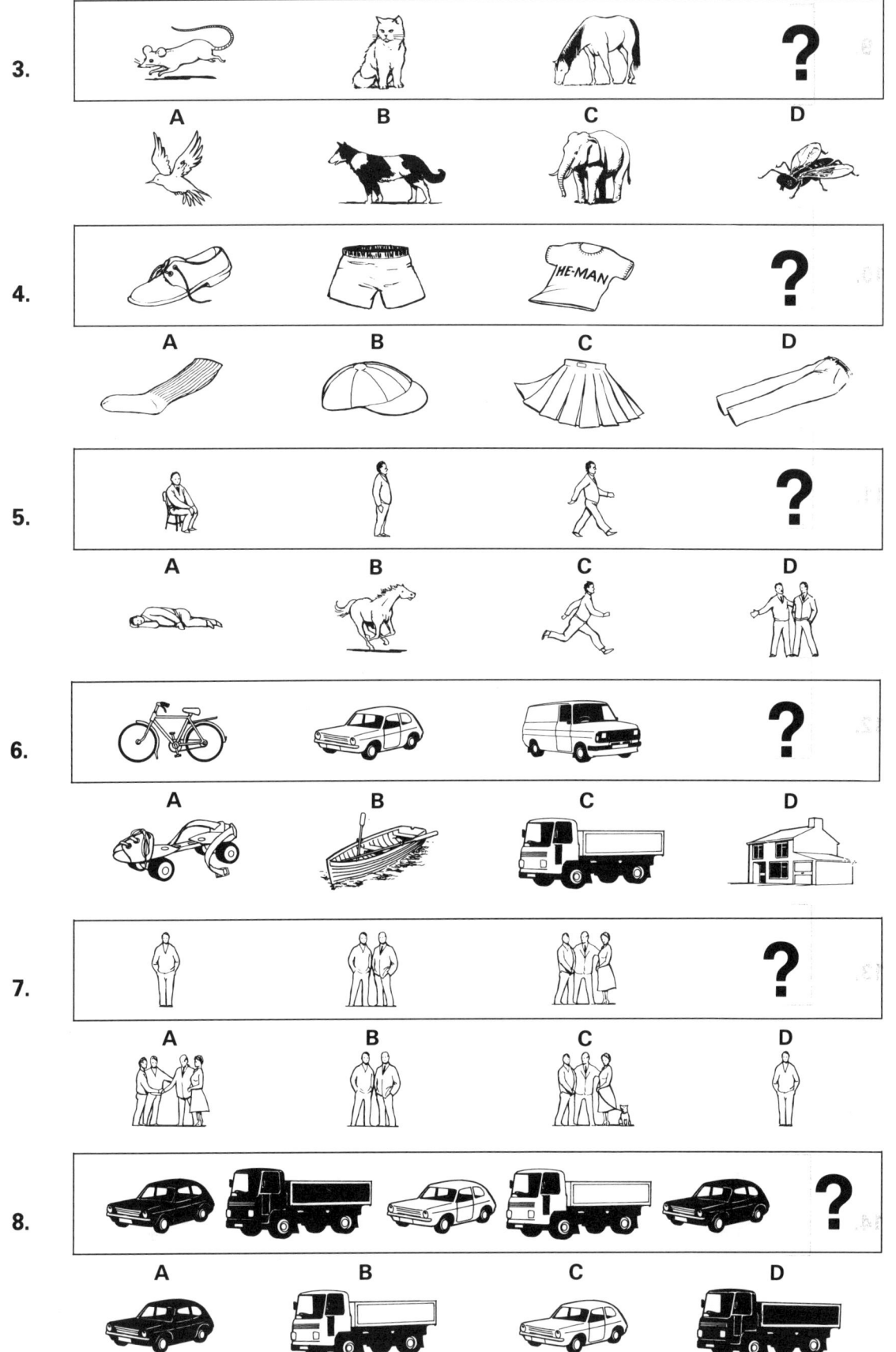

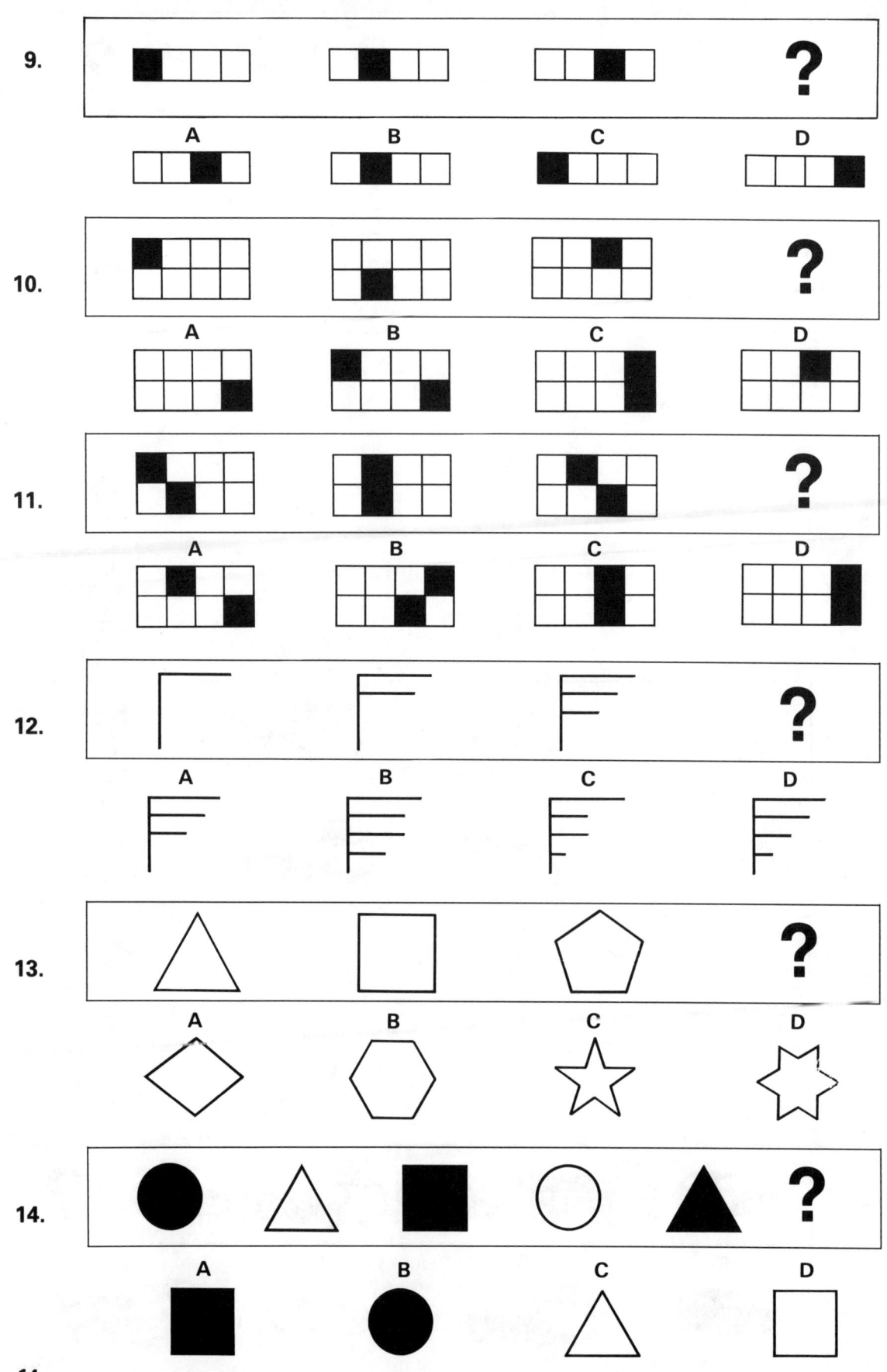

A note to parents

Important: read this before your child starts work.

About the tests
These tests are intended for children to complete with as little adult help as possible. The three areas – verbal, non-verbal and spatial – correspond to the most commonly assessed areas of reasoning. The units within each area allow the child to become familiar with the types of question often used in reasoning tests. The correct answer to each question is given in the answer key. You may wish to mark the child's work yourself, but the child could easily mark and correct some of the sections.
   The tests are not designed to enable you to compare the intelligence of the child with that of other children. You should consider the tests as useful reasoning test experience. Their main purpose is to familiarize a child with a range of different reasoning activities. This should help the child to show more fully what he or she can do if a more formal test is taken later on.

Getting the child started
Most children will need some help in starting to use the booklet. Approach the tests as a kind of game or quiz, making sure the questions are tackled seriously, but do not let the child become over-anxious about the results. There is no need to approach the units in any particular order, but spend a little time with the child at the beginning of each one to make sure that he or she has a grasp of what is required. There is no time limit for any of the units but you should encourage reasonably quick working since formal reasoning tests are usually strictly timed.

What to do when the child has finished a Unit
Use the answer key in this centre page pull-out to tick each correct answer. The total number of ticks may then be entered in the score box at the end of the unit.

How to use the Scores Table on page 28
This is designed to bring together the scores for all eight units. You may then find a total score for each of the three areas of reasoning. Be wary of considering relatively low scores in any particular area as a definite sign of weakness. The difficulty of the questions is different from area to area.

What to do about low scores
Children will vary greatly in their scores. While it is tempting to interpret these variations as differences in reasoning ability, it is important to realize that this is not necessarily true. Lack of familiarity with the types of question or with the method of answering can quite easily result in low scores. Remember that some children require more practice than others before they can show what they can really do. Some children may not do their best because they are over-anxious, whilst others may not have taken the tasks seriously enough. You cannot, therefore, take a low score as meaning that the child definitely has poor reasoning ability.
   If, however, the child does not score highly on any or all of the tests do not cause anxiety by expressing disappointment or by chastising. Take the opportunity to discuss wrong answers. This will help you understand how the child reasons, and will also help the child to understand what is required. If the child does not understand your explanations he or she may not be ready to complete the booklet. Perhaps they are too young or would benefit from other experiences, as suggested on page 3.

Sometimes a child will get a low score in one particular area. Perhaps there is a preference for spatial tasks rather than verbal ones, for example. Such differences as these help to demonstrate that reasoning is a complicated ability to understand. We all show a remarkable diversity of reasoning skills and we all have strengths and weaknesses. The skills tested here cannot hope to cover the whole range. Some children's best strengths will in fact lie outside the scope of this booklet.

Finally, you should remember that some units are generally more difficult than others. Low scores may be reflecting this rather than the child's level of ability. Some of the individual questions are also, purposefully, rather difficult so that all children will find some parts of the booklet a real challenge. Remember that no child is expected to get full marks. If you simply treat each unit as an experience of reasoning tasks from which the child can learn you will be making the most effective use of this booklet.

Further activities

No matter how well the child does, certain activities involving reasoning can be valuable as part of a child's general development. This does not mean that the questions in this booklet should be practised excessively. Simple familiarization with the types of question given here is normally sufficient to enable children to show their best ability when sitting formal tests. To develop the child's reasoning further you could encourage thinking in a variety of ways. Talking, questioning and playing can all help – especially if they involve challenges or novelties. Much of a child's ordinary school work requires reasoning and problem solving and so these kinds of activity should be encouraged. However, other activities for you to enjoy with the child are suggested on the inside back cover.

Remember, children learn better when they are not anxious and when things are enjoyable and fun. They also have a different view of the world which, as adults, we sometimes fail to understand. If they do not reason like we do it is quite normal. They will learn adult methods in due course. Like everything else, mature reasoning develops slowly and we should nurture its development, not force it on at too great a pace.

Answer Key

Unit One

1. C
2. A
3. D
4. B
5. A
6. B
7. C
8. A
9. D
10. D
11. B
12. A
13. D
14. D
15. B
16. C
17. A
18. C
19. A
20. D

Unit Two

1. pear
2. knee
3. Tuesday
4. dinner
5. feel
6. speak
7. spring
8. breeze
9. basin
10. stool
11. creek
12. cram
13. immense
14. stamp
15. sandal
16. newspaper
17. match
18. rage
19. idle
20. rough

Unit Three

1. foot
2. fruit
3. hear
4. night
5. hospital
6. chaos
7. avoid
8. neck
9. gallop
10. white
11. cry
12. wrist
13. feather
14. ball
15. mountain
16. colour
17. animal
18. time
19. forest
20. hail

Unit Four

1. C
2. B
3. C
4. B
5. C
6. C
7. A
8. D
9. D
10. A
11. C
12. D
13. B
14. D
15. A
16. A
17. B
18. C
19. A
20. C

Answer Key

Unit Five

1. A
2. B
3. C
4. B
5. B
6. D
7. C
8. D
9. A
10. B
11. D
12. D
13. C
14. B
15. D
16. C
17. A
18. D
19. A
20. B

Unit Six

1. C
2. B
3. A
4. C
5. C
6. D
7. A
8. B
9. B
10. A
11. D
12. D
13. C
14. B
15. A
16. B
17. A
18. D
19. A
20. C

Unit Seven

1. F
2. T
3. F
4. T
5. T
6. T
7. T
8. F
9. F
10. F
11. D
12. F
13. F
14. T
15. F
16. F
17. T
18. T
19. T
20. F
21. D
22. T
23. F
24. T
25. F
26. F
27. T
28. D
29. T
30. F

Unit Eight

1. A
2. C
3. B
4. A
5. N
6. B
7. D
8. E
9. C
10. E
11. B
12. A
13. C
14. N
15. D
16. D
17. A
18. A
19. D
20. E
21. D
22. E
23. A
24. N
25. C
26. E
27. B
28. B
29. D
30. B

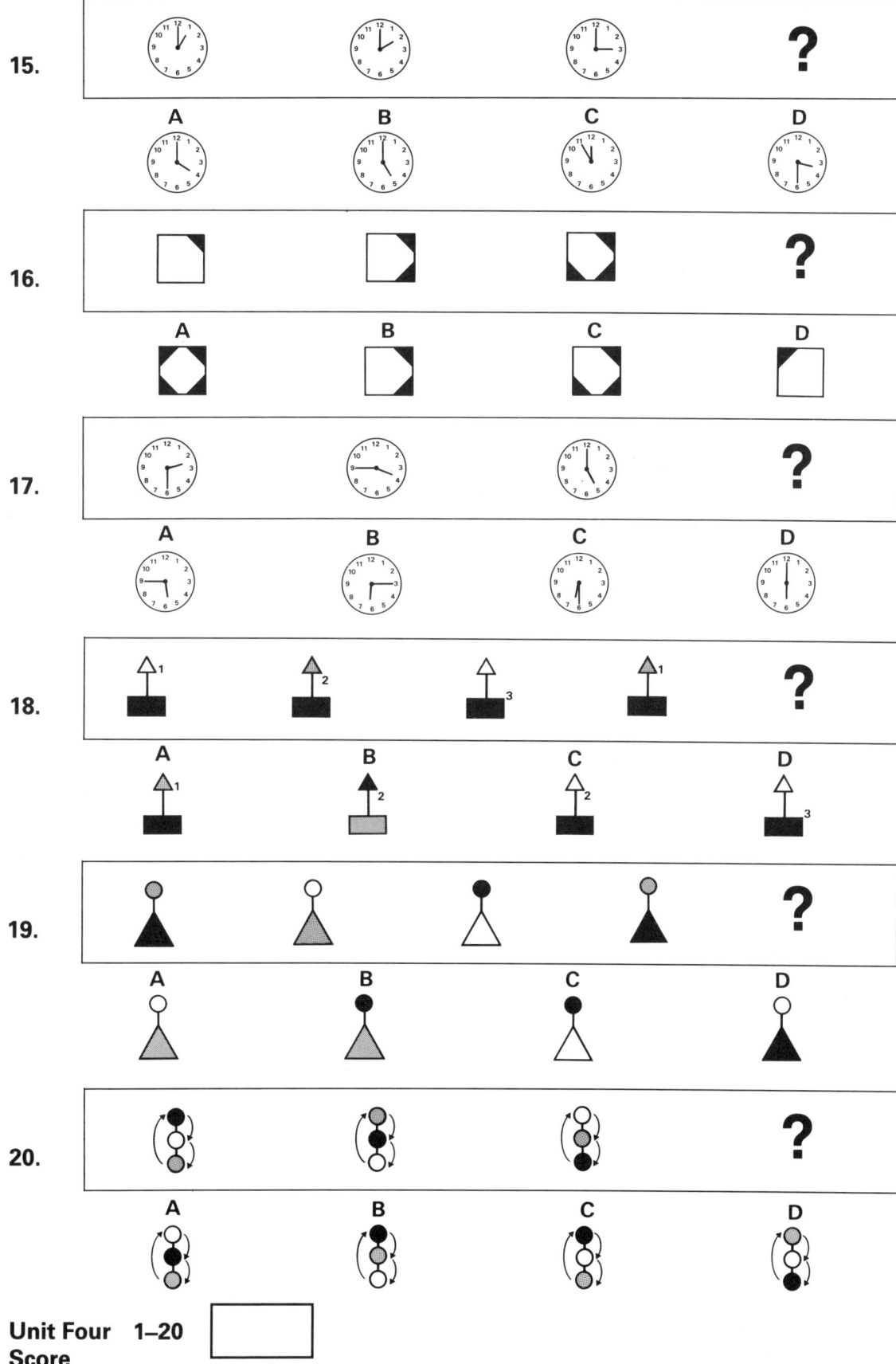

Unit Five

Look at these pictures.

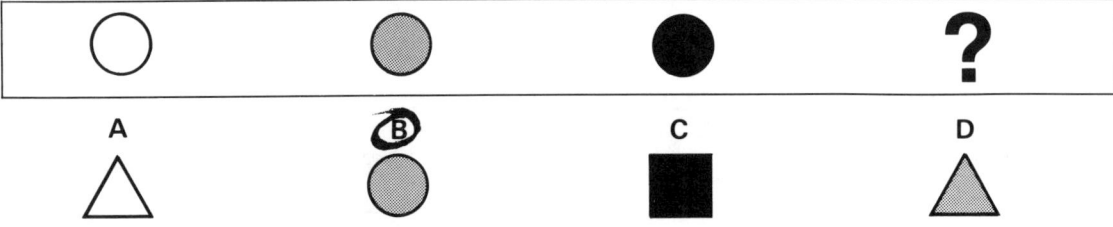

Which of the shapes A, B, C or D goes best with the three shapes inside the box? The answer is B because they are all circles. We have put a ring around B to show this. Now try this example.

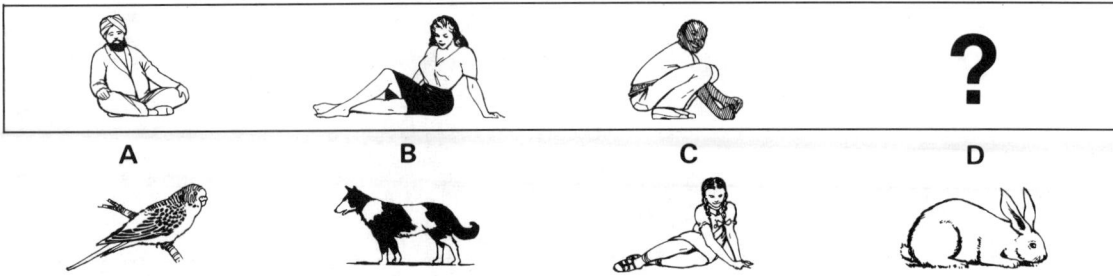

You should have put a ring around C because a girl is a person like a man, woman and a boy. If you got it wrong ask someone to explain. Otherwise begin the test.

Test Five starts here

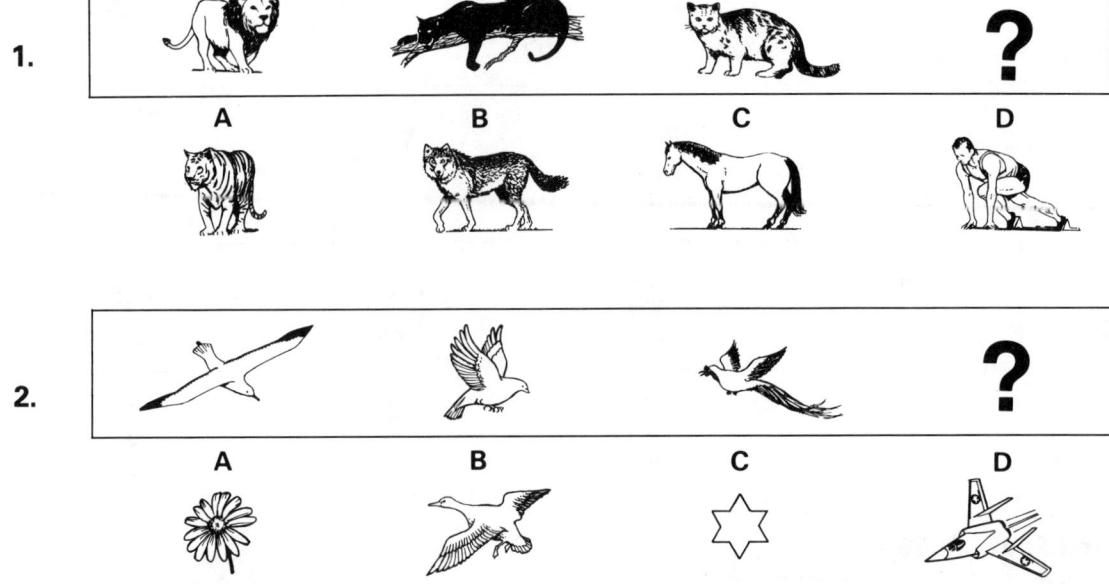

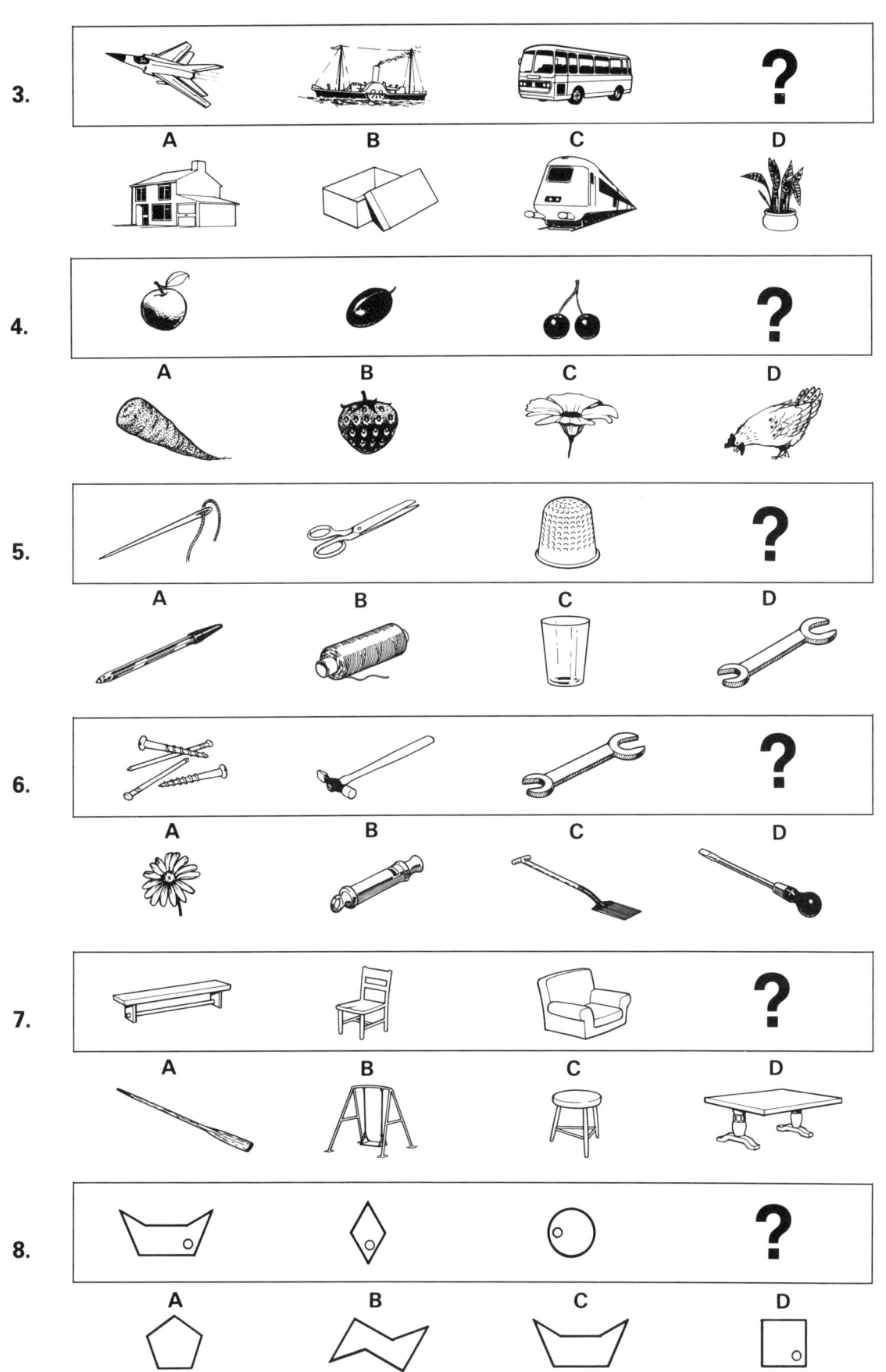

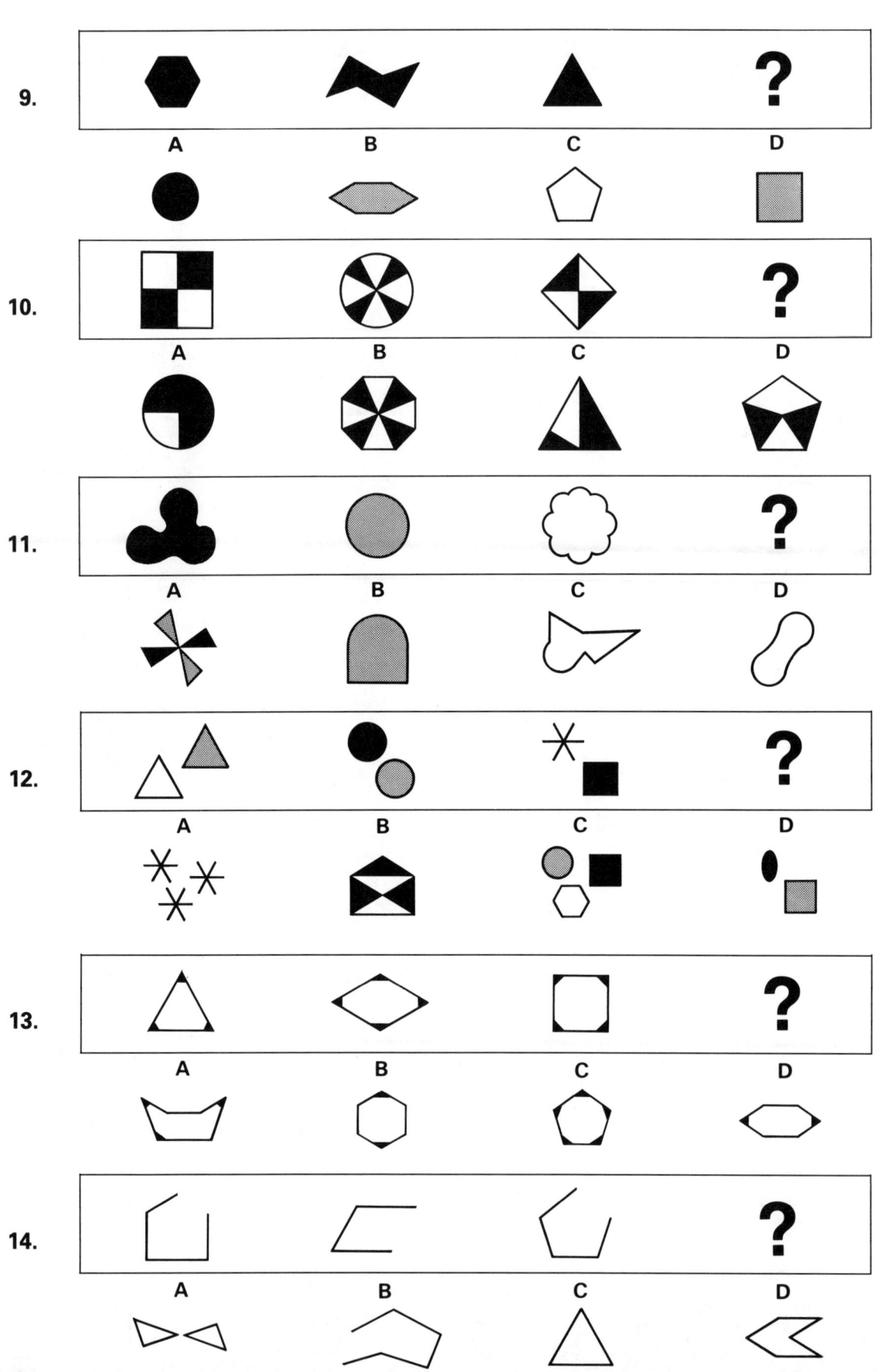

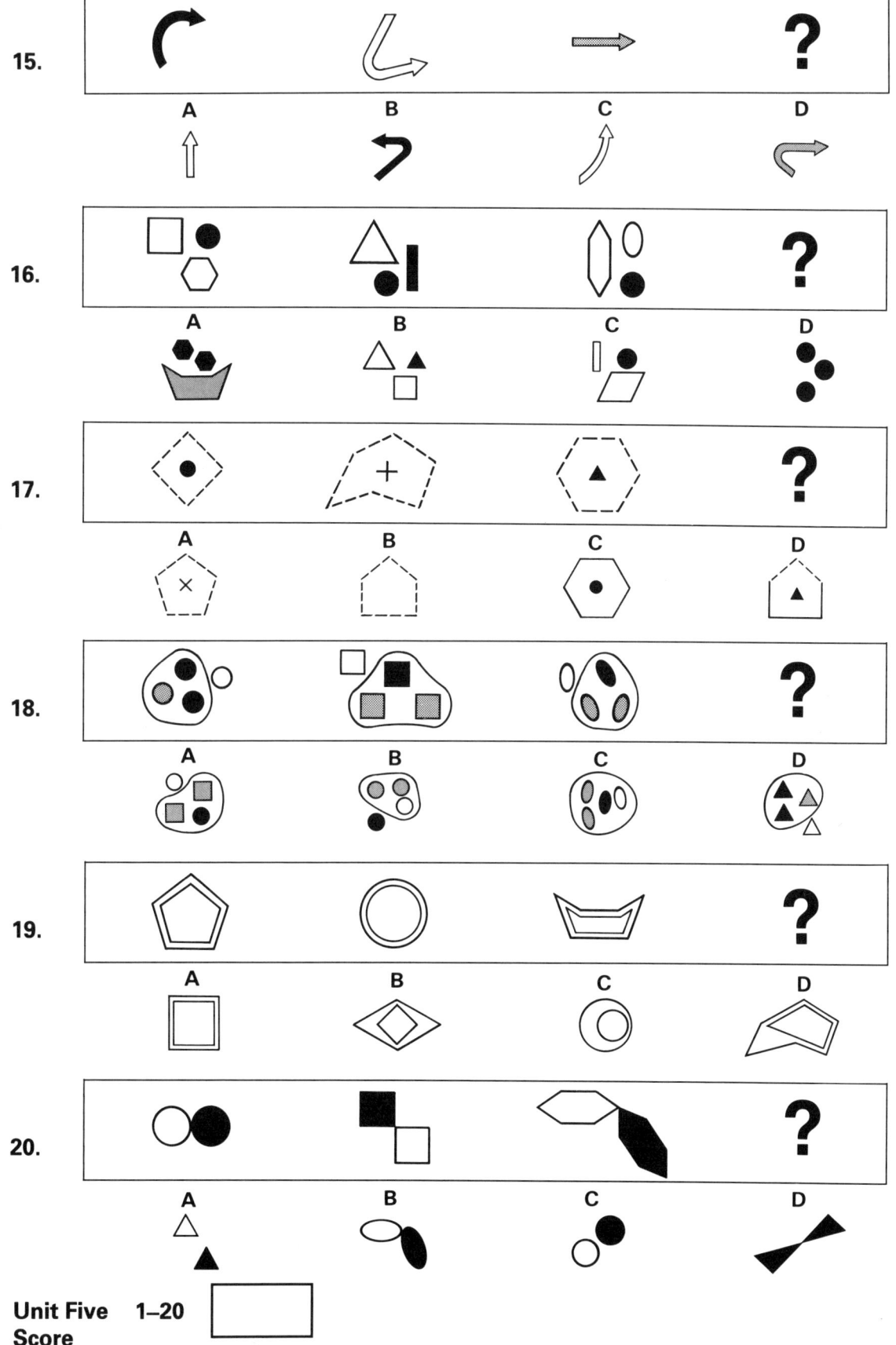

Unit Six

Look at these shapes.

Can you see that they go together in the same way?

In this test the questions will look like this:

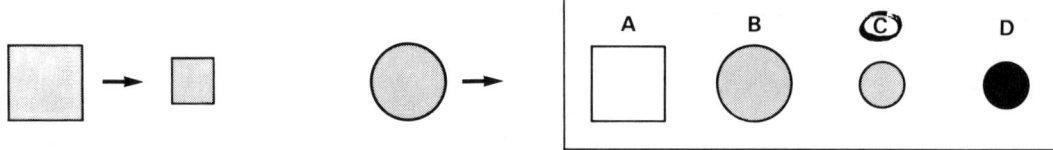

We have circled choice C, the small circle, to show that it goes with the big circle in the same way as the little square goes with the big square.

Now try this example and put a ring around your choice before reading on.

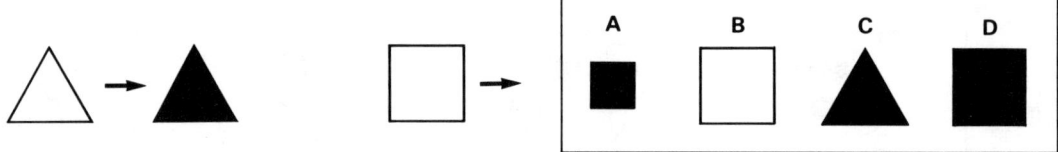

You should have chosen D. White Triangle to Black Triangle is like White Square to Black Square. If you are not sure ask someone to explain. Otherwise begin the test.

Test Six starts here

1.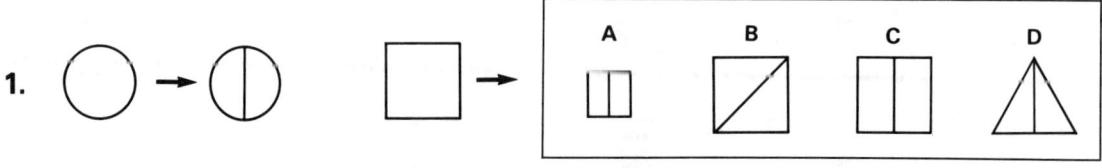

2.

20

3.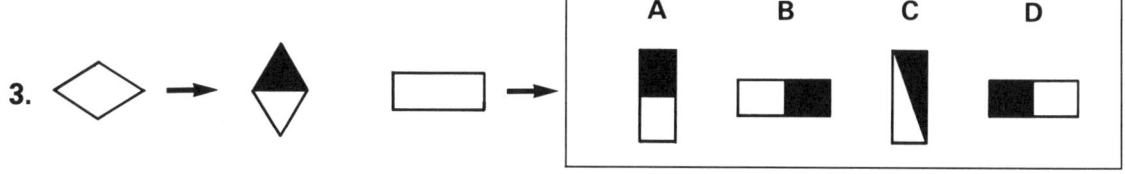

4.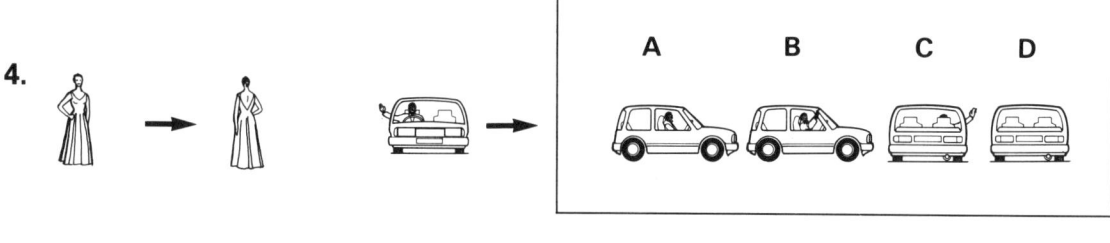

5.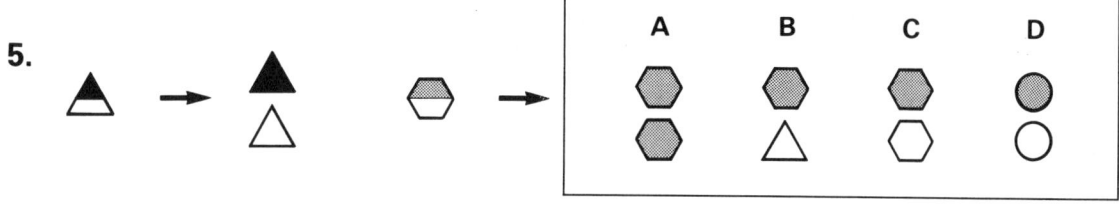

6.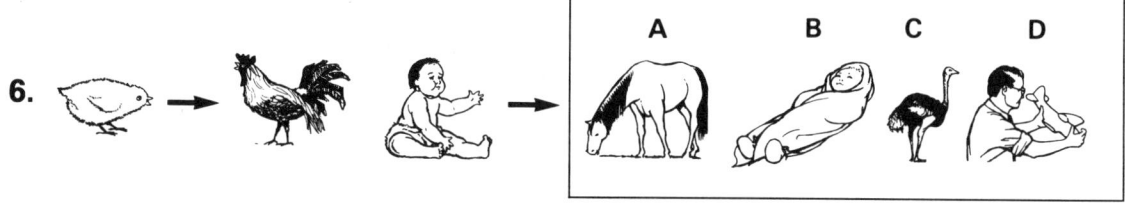

7.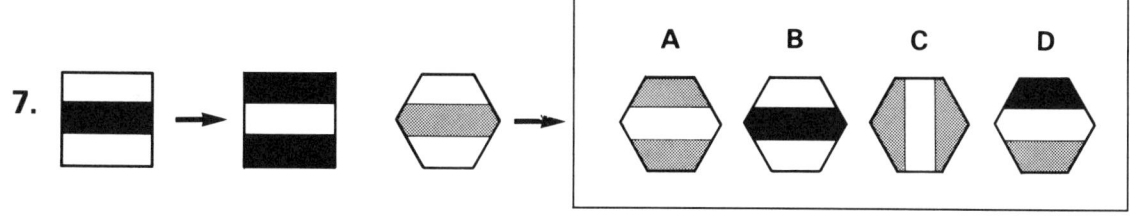

8.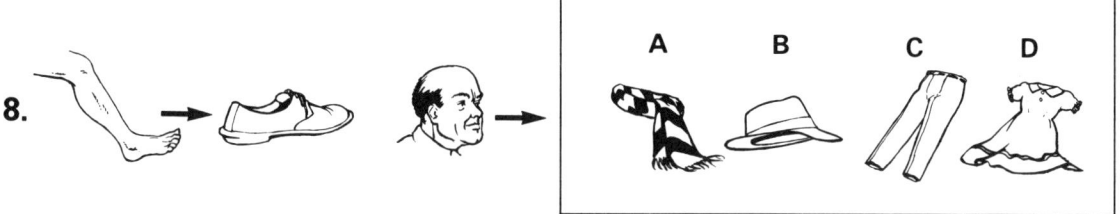

9.

 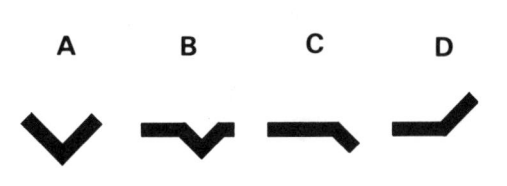

10.

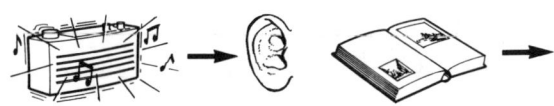 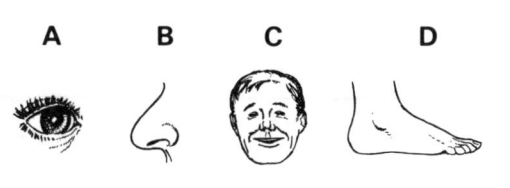

11.

 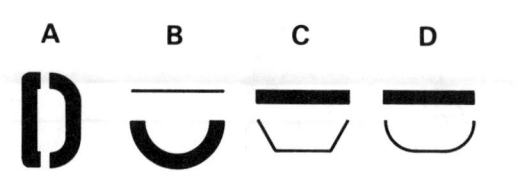

12.

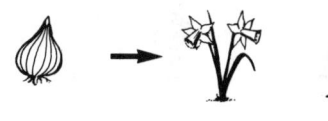 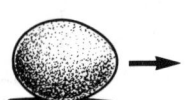 

13.

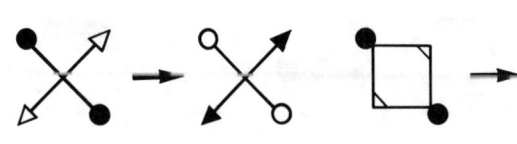 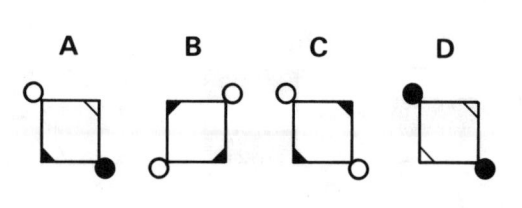

14.

 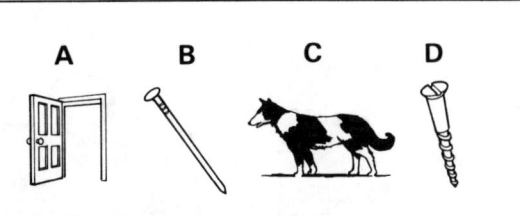

15.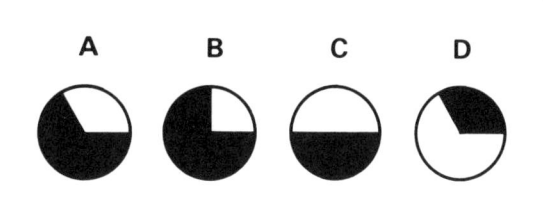

16.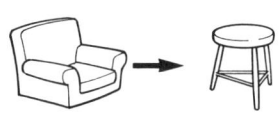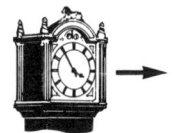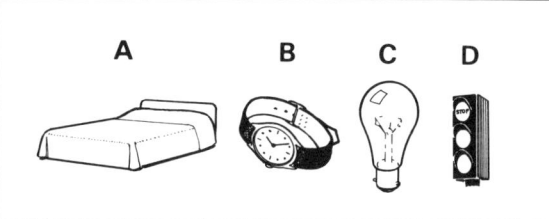

17.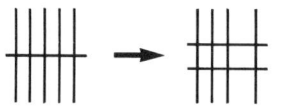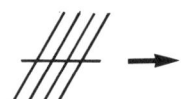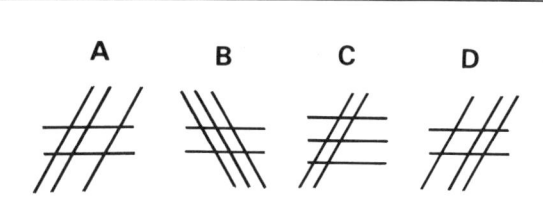

18.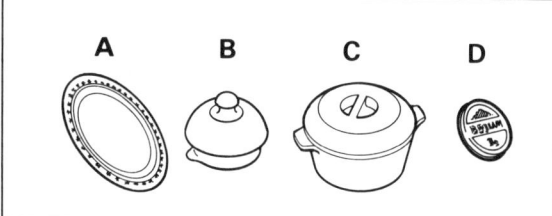

19.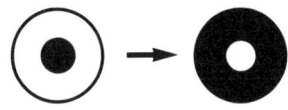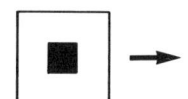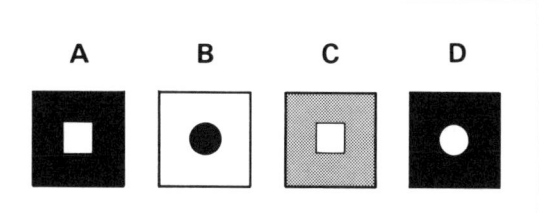

20.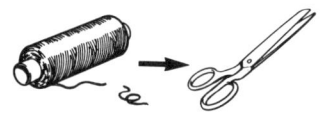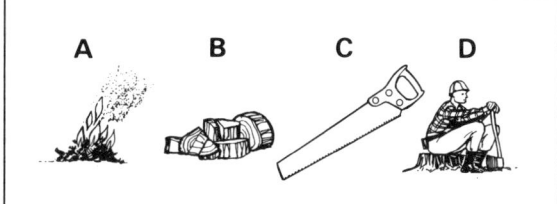

Unit Six Score 1–20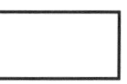

Unit Seven

Look at this shape.

Here it is again but it has been turned a bit.

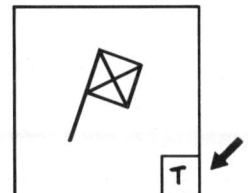

Here it is again but it has been flipped over. It cannot look like this simply by turning it.

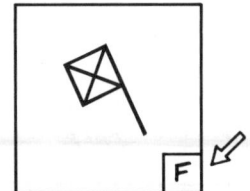

To show that a shape has been turned and not flipped we write T in the little box in the corner as shown by the black arrow. To show that a shape has been flipped over as well as turned we write F in the box in the corner as shown by the white arrow. If a shape has been changed we write D to show it is different.

In this test you must look at the shape on the left in the circle and decide which of the shapes in the boxes to its right have been turned (T), flipped (F) or is simply different (D). Try these examples. The first one has been done for you.

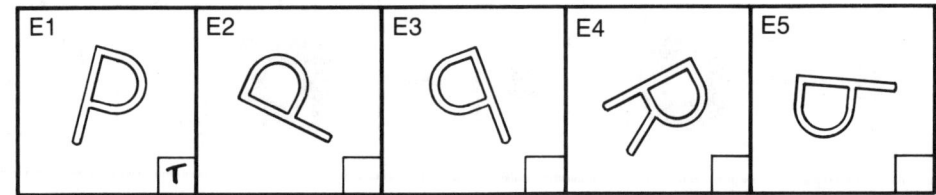

The answers are E2. T, E3. F, E4. D, E5. F. If you got any wrong ask someone to explain. Otherwise begin the test.

Remember:
  If the shape has been turned write T
  If the shape has been flipped write F
  If the shape has been turned and flipped write F
  If the shape has been changed write D

Test Seven starts here

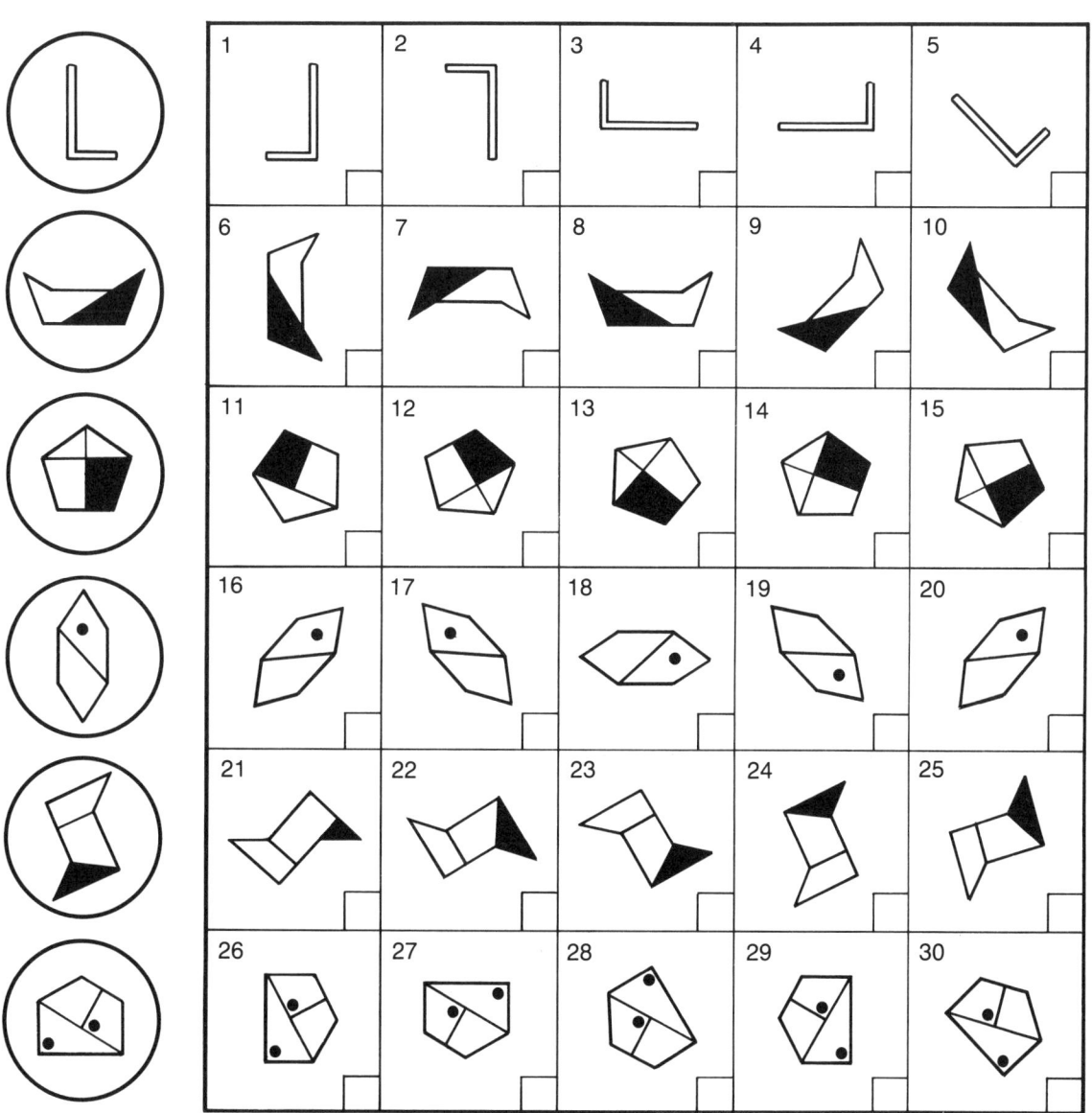

Unit Seven Score 1–30

Unit Eight

Look at these shapes.

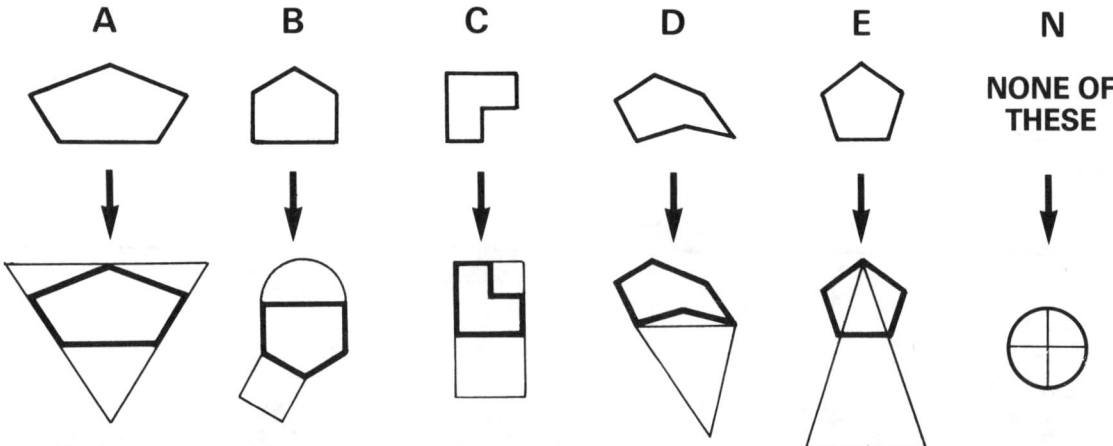

Can you see how each shape in the top row is hidden in the more complicated bottom figure? In this test you must decide which of the top shapes A, B, C, D or E is hidden in the figures in the test. The hidden shape must be the same size but it may have been turned around. Sometimes none of the shapes are hidden. You must write the letter A, B, C, D, E if you can see any of these shapes. Otherwise write N for none in the little box.

Try these examples. The first one has been done for you.

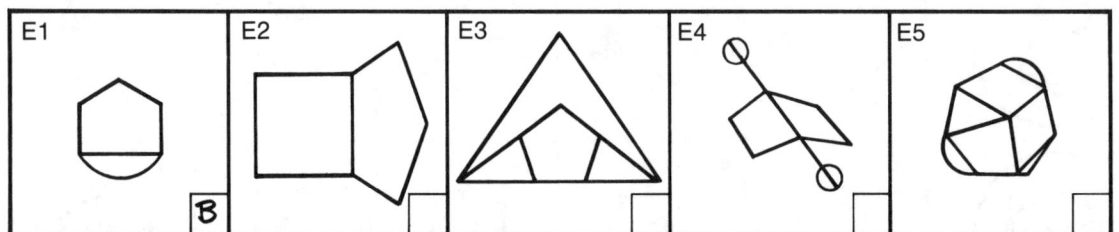

The answers are: E2) A E3) E E4) D E5) N

If you got any wrong ask someone to explain. Then begin the test. Remember to use the shapes at the top of the page.

Test Eight starts here

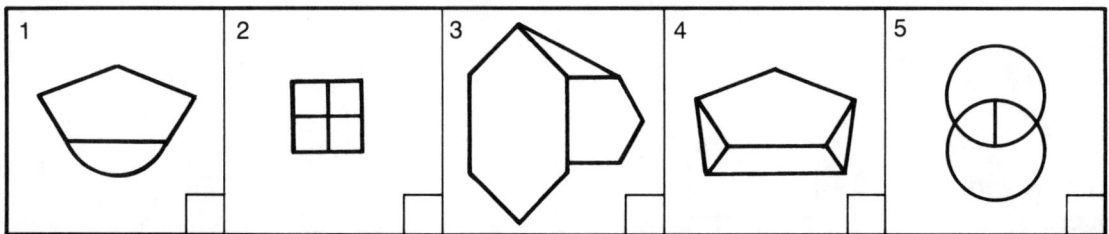

26

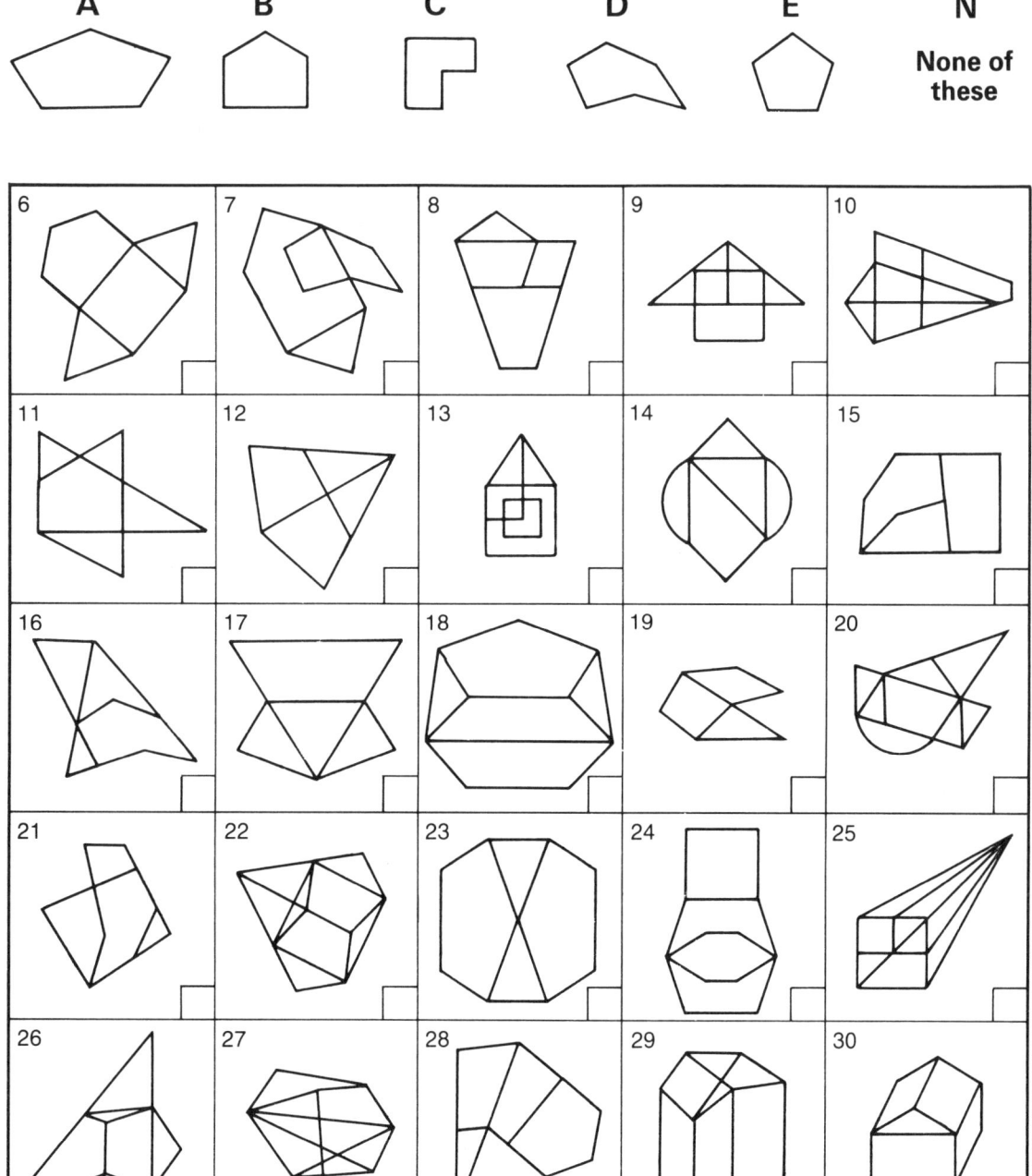

Scores Table

Unit	Description	Score	Totals
Verbal			
One	Vocabulary	.... Out of 20	**Verbal Total** .... Out of 60
Two	Classification	.... Out of 20	
Three	Analogies	.... Out of 20	
Non-verbal			
Four	Series	.... Out of 20	**Non-verbal Total** .... Out of 60
Five	Classification	.... Out of 20	
Six	Analogies	.... Out of 20	
Spatial			
Seven	Rotations and inversions	.... Out of 30	**Spatial Total** .... Out of 60
Eight	Embedded figures	.... Out of 30	